THE UNSPOKEN
TRUTH ABOUT
PRIVATIZATION

THE UNSPOKEN TRUTH ABOUT PRIVATIZATION

✦

Nine Essays

The "UNSPOKEN TRUTH" Series, No. 2

Peter E. Temu

iUniverse, Inc.

New York Lincoln Shanghai

THE UNSPOKEN TRUTH ABOUT PRIVATIZATION
Nine Essays

iUniverse books may be ordered through booksellers or by contacting:

iUniverse
2021 Pine Lake Road, Suite 100
Lincoln, NE 68512
www.iuniverse.com
1-800-Authors (1-800-288-4677)

Because of the dynamic nature of the Internet, any Web addresses or links contained in this book may have changed since publication and may no longer be valid.

The views expressed in this work are solely those of the author and do not necessarily reflect the views of the publisher, and the publisher hereby disclaims any responsibility for them.

ISBN: 978-0-595-47753-1

Printed in the United States of America

Contents

The 'UNSPOKEN TRUTH'
Series of Booklets
GENERAL FOREWORD TO
THE SERIES

By
Peter E. Temu

The Unspoken Truth booklets, to which this publication belongs, is a series of essays written in the full knowledge that they will be controversial. Big business, multilateral donors and dominant groups in society, to say nothing of governments, may find that the hidden truth exposed in these essays runs counter to their interests.

This series of booklets exposes the campaign of hypocrisy by vested interests which the world has tolerated for far too long. It is a campaign that relies on theories which have long been discredited and yet are deliberately invoked to prey on people whose poverty, fear and ignorance often prevent them from seeing the picture in its true perspective.

The Unspoken Truth booklets are not research monographs, unveiling new truths. They are merely bold re-statements of certain home truths, to which theory, experience, common sense and empirical findings bear ample testimony. But these truths are unpopular and are often glossed over because they run counter to powerful vested interests.

INTRODUCTION

The economy of any country may be said to consist of two sectors: the public sector, which is under the control of the government, and the private sector, which is under the control of private individuals or companies. Privatization is the policy or process of converting, wholly or partially, public enterprises to private enterprises. It follows that during privatization, the relative share of the private sector in the national economy expands, and that of the public sector contracts.

This book consists of nine short essays on the following topics:

- The rationale for the existence of a public sector
- The rationale for the existence of a private sector
- The rationale for privatization
- The process of privatization
- Striking the right balance between the public and the private sector.
- Privatization and 'Foreignization'
- Privatize at any cost?
- Privatization: Ownership *versus* Management
- Privatization in Tanzania: A Case Study

Though often defended on economic and ideological grounds, privatization is a highly sensitive political issue. This fact is more readily appreciated if we consider, not just privatization, but its converse, nationalization. Seemingly, the two phenomena are diametrically opposite, and mutually exclusive. Yet, they are closely interrelated. An understanding of the one sheds light on an understanding of the other, and pronouncements on both can be made in the same breath.

Unfortunately, there is a tendency, especially in developing or newly independent countries, to identify—and to exploit for political ends—the sensitivities surrounding foreign ownership, by deliberately confusing it with privatization. The case for privatization is sometimes diluted by vote-seeking politicians, who have forged the term 'foreignization', in order to invoke nationalist sentiments by misleading their voters into believing that privatization meant surrendering national sovereignty to rich foreigners.

Though addressed in two separate essays, the rationale for the existence of a public sector and the rationale for the existence of a private sector are each other's mirror image. The 'grey area' between them—which seeks to define where the public sector ends and the private sector begins—is the real crux of this presentation, and forms a separate essay of its own.

There is also a short essay devoted to an articulation of the distinction between ownership and management (or control) of economic enterprises. A careful examination of this distinction is essential to a proper understanding of the various forms and approaches to which the process of privatization is subject.

These preliminary essays, between them, should help the reader to see privatization in its proper perspective. They enable the discussion to proceed, as it should, within a properly defined historical and institutional context, to arrive at meaningful conclusions.

Whether privatization is useful or harmful is largely an empirical question—to be answered, not on the basis of political dogma, but of a sober and detached examination of the circumstances surrounding each specific case.

Essay # 1
THE RATIONALE FOR THE EXISTENCE OF A PUBLIC SECTOR.

As the term implies, the public sector is there to serve the public interest. Government, as an institution, is the natural custodian of the public sector.

All the goods produced and services rendered by the government for the benefit of its citizens are part and parcel of the public sector.

At this level of generality, there is little to dispute. On reflection, however, certain questions do arise. For example: does the government—*any* government—necessarily or automatically serve the public interest? At what cost? And what is the 'public interest' anyway?

These questions are debatable because they border partly on the philosophical, and partly on the empirical. As such, they have no clear-cut answers. Nevertheless, they are absolutely of the essence and have to be addressed.

Government as a human institution has existed, in some shape or form, from time immemorial. The way governments perceive their role in society and exercise their authority often differs from country to country, from generation to generation, and even from one historical epoch to another. Down the ages, governments have been accepted—or tolerated—because of their ability to enforce law and order, and to defend their citizens against external attack. These basic obligations confer on all governments the sovereign right to have armed forces and courts of justice, and the right

3

to levy taxes and raise revenues with which to finance the legislative, judicial and administrative machinery of the state.

The reason why such functions are—and are destined to remain—the responsibility of governments is because it is impossible in civil society for a private individual to guarantee his own safety and security, and to enjoy the fruits of his labour free from fear, harassment or interference from others. Whether we like it or not, people's lives are interdependent. We are all subject to conventional social, cultural and legal norms of behaviour. Society must be protected from—and be able to punish—criminals and wrong-doers, both from within its own ranks and from outside its own community.

The bottom line, or irreducible minimum, of government involvement—that is, a minimum size for the public sector—is therefore generally recognised, and attracts little controversy.

There is, however, a whole range of activities in which governments tend to get involved, more because of their lust for power and love of prestige, than because of any compelling social necessity. These are the kinds of activities which private individuals or companies could do just as well, if not better. From country to country, or generation to generation, and depending on one's political perception, ideas differ as to what should be the proper limits of public involvement in the social, economic and cultural lives of the people.

For instance, should governments be responsible for the construction and maintenance of roads and railways, harbours and airports? Are social services, such as health and education, and the provision of goods and infrastructure which they entail, proper matters for the private sector or for the public sector? How about basic scientific and technological research? Above all, could government not accept responsibility for any or all of these tasks, and still leave their actual management to private individuals?

These types of questions pose a unique challenge, and are at the core of the privatization debate. The way we answer them tends to differ according to our social circumstances and our political orientation.

Precisely because the dividing line between what ought to fall within the public sector and what ought to fall within the private sector is not so clear, privatization will always remain a controversial issue. The pros and cons have to be weighed carefully in any given situation in order to strike the right balance, and avoid the unfortunate tendency to make stereotype decisions which are based more on political dogma than on objective reality.

Consider, for instance, countries under socialist regimes, such as China, Russia, some in Eastern Europe, plus some in Africa, Latin America and the Caribbean, where central planning is of paramount importance. Because of their political orientation, these countries naturally have a proportionately larger public sector than do countries under capitalist regimes such as the United States and Western Europe. Indeed, that is the very feature that distinguishes them from the capitalist countries.

Yet, even in the Western capitalist countries, significant differences do exist in the extent and nature of their privatization. In the United Kingdom, for example, the Conservative Government under Margaret Thatcher went much farther in its pursuit of privatization than the Labour Party would have wished. Likewise, the privatization agenda of the United States Republicans goes far beyond what would be acceptable to the Democrats.

The rationale for the existence and operations of the public sector may therefore be construed as falling under two broad heads:

- First, a relatively conservative and non-controversial area, which entails governments' traditional functions and responsibilities to its people—defence, maintenance of law and order, and the public administration machinery necessary in the execution of those functions;

- Second, a fairly controversial area—the 'grey area', so to speak—where, for quite legitimate reasons, opinions differ, depending on the social, political, economic and cultural orientation of the society in question.

Needless to say, it is this 'grey area' that much of the debate on privatization revolves around. And it is precisely here that powerful vested interests keep asserting themselves, and political dogmatism is most in evidence.

In the following pages, we shall try to avoid preconceptions as much as possible and deal with privatization as soberly and objectively as we can. In this way, we can face the truth—*the unspoken truth*—boldly and squarely, as the well-known, but less popular, aspects of the subject are laid bare.

Essay # 2
THE RATIONALE FOR THE EXISTENCE OF A PRIVATE SECTOR

The existence of a private sector is a practical demonstration of man's inalienable right to 'freedom, liberty and the pursuit of happiness'. In a free society, men and women have the right to perform, in their private capacity, any legitimate activity—economic, social, cultural, or religious—either alone or in company, without fear of interference from the government. It is these private pursuits which, in their totality, constitute the private sector of the economy.

At the level of organized society, what economists call a 'free market economy' sums up the interactions of individuals—producers and consumers—within the private sector. The seller of any commodity seeks the highest profit, while the buyer seeks maximum utility or the best value for his money. Any seller is free to sell or not to sell, and any buyer is free to buy or not to buy. When both sides enter into a transaction, they do so voluntarily, by mutual consent, and to their mutual satisfaction.

What is true of one producer or consumer is true, in principle, of all producers and consumers, the only difference being that individuals tend to differ in their personal tastes as well as in their natural and economic endowments, including purchasing power. Differences in these individual attributes are natural, understandable, and perfectly acceptable, and do not detract in any way from the fact that everyone in the market is at liberty to pursue his own interests.

What is more, the price at which goods and services in such a market are bought and sold—what is called the *'equilibrium price'*—depends on the forces of supply and demand in the market as a whole, and not on the whim of any public authority, power, or influence of any particular individual or group.

This is the economic model of perfect competition, a model dating back to the days of eighteenth century classical economists. Though not always openly acknowledged, the theory still holds sway in contemporary economic and political circles, and exerts considerable influence on the thinking of public officials in Western countries.

The main attraction of the theory lies in the fact that a precise parallel can be drawn between the free market model and the liberal democracy mindset, whereby the 'consumer' in a free market corresponds to the 'voter' in a democracy.

If, in a free market economy, so goes the argument, the consumer is king, in a Western-type democracy, the voter is supreme. Just as the consumer is free to spend (or not to spend) his dollars on a given commodity, so the voter is free to vote (or not to vote) for a given candidate. Central to both scenarios is the *freedom to choose*.

However, the analogy between the economic scenario and the political scenario, though meaningful, must not be pushed too far. It does not hold for poor developing countries, nor for countries under autocratic regimes with few democratic freedoms. More by default than by design, such countries may have a sizeable private sector, either because of poverty and underdevelopment, or because their autocratic rulers are more obsessed with amassing wealth for themselves, than they are with their people's economic welfare.

It is therefore a mistake to assume that the larger the private sector in a given country, the more democratic the regime. Sometimes the converse may be true. The rationale for the existence of a private sector, as well as its nature and size, are empirical questions which cannot be answered in the abstract.

Depending on the context, the rationale for the existence of a private sector may therefore be viewed in either of two ways:

- In a modern state, typified by a Western democracy, the existence of a large and expanding private sector is a mark of the degree to which people are free to exercise their political and economic liberties;

- In a typical developing country, the subsistence sector is in fact the private sector *par excellence;* while in an authoritarian or otherwise undemocratic regime, the existence of a sizeable private sector may merely be a reflection of the fact that the regime does not care much about what its own people are doing to make a living. In either case, the size of the private sector has little to do with the presence or absence of democracy.

In a nutshell: privatization, and the existence of a large private sector, may be a necessary condition—but certainly not a sufficient condition—for democracy. Many African countries which, under pressure from external donors, have hastened to privatize (or de-nationalize) their enterprises, without first weighing the consequences, are having to learn this lesson the hard way.

Essay # 3
THE RATIONALE FOR PRIVATIZATION

Privatization is the expression of a policy which seeks to give the people decisive control over the ownership and management of their economic resources. Countries in which privatization has been successfully accomplished, or is still being actively pursued, are variously referred to as *private enterprise* or *free enterprise* economies.

The move from a state-controlled economy to a free enterprise economy—in other words, privatization—is often advocated, and rightly defended, on the grounds of efficiency and cost-effectiveness. The elimination of various forms of government control is seen as a way of ensuring that both consumers and producers enjoy the freedom of choice that is needed for the efficient operation of a market economy. From outright ownership and control, to the regulation of prices and wages, and the levying of taxes and subsidies—government interference in the economy can take a wide variety of different forms. Their purposeful elimination is the whole motive behind privatization.

The assumption that a private enterprise economy is better at 'delivering the goods' than a centrally planned (or government-controlled) economy is firmly rooted in economic theory and borne out by practical experience. Like all theoretical models, the model that demonstrates the inherent superiority of perfect competition over monopolistic or other forms of production, marketing and distribution rests on certain simplifying assumptions. These assumptions include the existence of:

- Perfect knowledge among producers and consumers

- Perfect mobility of resources

- Freedom to enter and leave the industry

- Producers seeking maximum profits, and consumers maximum satisfaction

- Both producers and consumers being free from public interference

- Both producers and consumers being 'price takers'; each too small to influence the market.

In the real world, of course, many of these assumptions do not hold true. Perfect knowledge does not exist. Nor is existing knowledge—or the 'state of the arts'—equally well known, let alone equally shared, among producers; hence the widespread presence of patents, trade marks and laws to protect 'intellectual property'. Many productive resources are both limited in quantity, and fixed or immobile. Producers (and to some extent consumers), far from being small or weak and unable to influence the market, are in fact organized into entities which are sometimes so large and influential that their power has to be controlled, if not curbed, by the state (hence the existence of laws against mergers and monopolies).

Still, when account has been taken of all these factors, the fact remains that in the modern world the free market model and its conclusions still hold sway in influential circles, and continue to be regarded, particularly in the Western world, as if it was the way forward for any country truly committed to democracy.

Herein then lies the rationale for privatization. It is based on the belief that the ideal economy is that which most closely approximates the free market model. Such an economy, it is said, is consistent with the existence of democratic liberties and the exercise of the freedom of choice on the part of producers and consumers. It is therefore argued that centrally planned economies need to be decentralized, liberalized and democratized; and to achieve these ends, they have to be privatized.

It is therefore not surprising that in a world currently dominated by Western ideology, and largely dependent on Western donor aid, privatization is widely embraced. Arguments against it do crop up, but they are often muted or given lip service, and then quietly discarded as if they were the 'exceptions that proved the rule'.

Today, many agreements with donors openly stipulate the privatization of public enterprises as one of the conditions—or *conditionalities* as they are sometimes called—for funds being disbursed to recipient countries, particularly in Africa. The agreements lay down that the actual disbursement of funds, from year to year, will be conditional on a demonstration of satisfactory progress in the privatization of the economy from one phase to the next.

The strings attached to such aid are seen as a way of compelling the recipient countries to 'stay on the democratic course'.

The assumption that privatization automatically implies democratization has one inherent weakness: it neglects the need for careful prior analysis of the pros and cons of each individual act of privatization. When undertaken, an analysis of that kind invariably reveals no automatic link between democracy and privatization. What ultimately counts is the form that privatization takes, how well it is designed, and the manner in which it is implemented.

Essay # 4
THE PROCESS OF PRIVATIZATION

To begin with, it must be presumed that the activity to be privatized is initially in public hands, otherwise the question of privatizing it would not, of course, arise. But once we have decided on privatization, the next question is exactly how to go about it; for, the process of privatization can be just as important as the end result.

Privatization can be approached in many different ways, each of which has its own merits and demerits. The way we go about it with respect to one activity or sector may—and for good reasons—differ from the way we go about it with respect to another.

Take the transport sector, for example. In many countries, public transportation plays an important role, alongside private transportation. In the case of road and rail transport, the reason why both public companies and private ones operate simultaneously in the same country is because certain routes are much less profitable than others. The routes with heavier passenger traffic are attractive to private operators whose primary motive is to maximize profits, but those with sparse traffic are shunned by private operators because they are less profitable or may actually be loss-making.

Generally, you will not find public companies operating along the same routes, in competition with private ones. The reason is not that public companies are less interested in making money. Rather, it is because their public licence requires them to serve those customers who happen to live in remote, less developed, peripheral and relatively inaccessible areas. These areas are not profitable enough to attract private operators, and yet the government, as a matter of policy, would not like the inhabitants living in these marginal and disadvantaged areas to feel that they were being neglected or discriminated against in the provision of such an essential service.

If the government decides to privatize the entire transport sector, therefore, it has to implement the policy in a way that convinces the private operator that running a bus or train service to remote areas of the country will be a paying proposition. And the only way to ensure that his profit will be the same, or at least comparable, with that of his counterparts on the more profitable routes will be by granting him a subsidy (or tax concession) enough to bridge the difference.

This kind of privatization, then, necessarily leans heavily on public support. It is resorted to where society does not believe that running a transport business, for example, should be the proper function of the state; although society is perfectly willing to let the state use its fiscal powers, in the public interest, to channel revenue from the more profitable routes in order to subsidise the less profitable ones.

This example typifies those cases where governments are involved in social and economic activities of various kinds, which society considers desirable or necessary, but which in themselves are unlikely to attract profit-motivated private individuals.

There are a good many cases, however, where governments are engaged in a variety of social and economic activities in direct competition with—or to the exclusion of—perfectly able and willing private operators. This is where the *economic* case for privatization is strongest, and where governments raise the spectre of *nationalism* as the political justification for engaging in those activities.

Later on in this presentation, we shall try to demonstrate that nationalization and privatization are not necessarily mutually exclusive. For the moment, however, we continue to focus attention on the privatization process. What form of privatization is appropriate, assuming that a decision to privatize (in other words, de-nationalize) has been reached?

In the first place, there may be some state corporations (commonly referred to as 'parastatals') that own and operate various types of businesses—flour mills, cattle ranches, commercial banks, tourist resorts, etc.

Such parastatals could be privatized wholesale: auctioned or sold 'as is' to the highest bidder. Provided there is no rigging, favouritism or corruption, this competitive bidding is all that the privatization process requires. The process should yield good results—the ablest and most efficient private operators would take over the industries and, hopefully, operate them more efficiently and more profitably than the parastatals they replaced.

Secondly, there may be cases where such a private take-over is not desirable, and where the privatization process must not be allowed to be so free and unrestrained. Consider, for instance, the provision of an essential service such as water supply, sewage disposal, electric power, and telecommunication services for a major city. These are typical cases where privatization may be called for, in the interests of efficiency, but where the process has to follow some slightly different rules, under public supervision, in the interests of social equity.

It follows that the highest bidder is not necessarily the most acceptable. The successful bidder should be the one who, while he is able to run the business profitably, also stands ready to make some sacrifice or concession in the public interest, should the occasion demand. This goes beyond reaching out to relatively marginal and disadvantaged areas; it includes confronting such challenges as an unexpected disruption of services (power cuts, minor flooding, a threatening epidemic outbreak, etc). Unless confronted early by a responsible and duty-bound private operator, these challenges could quickly degenerate into major national disasters requiring emergency action, at great public expense both financially and in human lives.

The government may therefore feel obliged, in privatizing services of this kind, to prescribe terms which give the privatization process a 'human touch'. This type of privatization is a form of *partial* privatization, since the private individual (or corporation) does not have unfettered freedom to do as he wants purely for his own personal gain.

Partial privatization is intended to combine the advantages of both state ownership and private ownership. It subtends the 'grey area', referred to earlier, lying between the public sector and the private sector, where the two sectors are partly intertwined. As such, the privatization process appropriate to it is not governed by any simple formula. It just calls for a solution that is tailor-made to suit each individual case, given the need to take into consideration the welfare interests of the wider community.

Thus, in a highly developed country with adequate infrastructure, a fairly dense population, well-educated people with high incomes, there may be little need for government interference in the private sector, beyond the levying of taxes and subsidies, plus a minimum of regulations to govern health standards, environmental protection, public security, and the like.

In a less developed country, however, to say nothing of a less developed country *under an authoritarian regime,* things are likely to be quite different. For one thing, the private sector might not be capable, given its poor skills and managerial ability, to successfully run a parastatal corporation. For another, because of poverty, poor technology, and the lack of infrastructure, the cost to any private operator of providing the product or service in question may well be beyond his reach. This means that the drive towards privatization will be slowed down, and the role of the public sector in providing basic necessities will be correspondingly increased.

There is a further implication. In view of the relatively poor state of the economy, including inadequate infrastructure and lack of investment resources, privatization, if it is pursued at all, may have to depend increasingly on foreign resources. This fact is very much in evidence in African countries today. But, for countries which were under the shackles of colonialism only a few decades ago, it is not surprising that privatization which is foreign-investment dependent, whatever its merits, is a politically sensitive issue, because it is portrayed by some as a partial surrender of national independence.

In such cases, it is imperative that the privatization exercise, to succeed, be handled with extra care—a point to which we shall return.

Probably, the best illustration of this relates to the mining sector. Typically, mining enterprises are capital intensive. Mineral prospecting alone requires a lot of initial expenditure, and the exploration itself may take years to bear fruit. Add to this the actual mining operations—the excavation, processing, and refining—all of which demand both skills and capital. The final product then needs to have a profitable market outlet before the initial expenses can be recouped, and surplus profits generated for distribution to shareholders.

Given the cost and the complexity of the exercise, and the time the entire process takes, it is not unusual for more than one company to be involved. For example, the company that does the initial prospecting may be different, with entirely different concessionary terms, from the company that undertakes the actual mining.

All this has direct implications for privatization—as further elaborated in the essay on "Privatization and 'Foreignization'.

Some unscrupulous foreign companies, especially in the service sectors such as hotels and tourism, take unfair advantage of the concessions they are granted. Tax holidays, in particular, are liable to repeated abuse. A foreign company comes in, runs its business rigorously during the initial tax-holiday period, makes a 'quick buck', and then pulls out on one pretext or another—only to return in the guise of a "new" entrepreneur, ready to enjoy the same tax holiday and profit repatriation privileges all over again!

In this connection, the frequency with which foreign-owned luxury hotels keep changing hands (and changing names) in African countries must be viewed with suspicion, especially since many of them have the same shareholders and overlapping directorships.

To minimise the risk of this kind of abuse becoming rampant, governments have to choose a form of privatization that is suitably tailored to meet the challenge. One way is out-contracting: competent foreigners are offered management contracts, while the control and ownership of the enterprise is retained by the government in the public interest.

In this way, the efficient running of the enterprise is guaranteed, while the retention of ownership in national hands eliminates the need for massive concessions in the form of tax holidays and profit repatriation, and all the temptations that go with them.

But there is a price to be paid. By virtue of its ownership, the government must provide the capital required to run the enterprise, although it is free to raise some of it locally and some from foreign sources. As time goes on, the government may decide, in its discretion, to relinquish or divest more and more of its own shareholding in favour of the private sector, in line with its privatization policy. The ownership stake of its own citizenry therefore is thereby increased, at a time when managerial control is still contracted out to foreigners. In time, steadily but surely, the managerial function, too, will pass to private nationals. At the end of the day, full privatization of the enterprise will have been achieved via this rather unconventional but well orchestrated process.

Essay # 5
STRIKING THE RIGHT BALANCE BETWEEN THE PUBLIC SECTOR AND THE PRIVATE SECTOR

It is clear that privatization can take many forms, proceed at different paces, and encounter varying degrees of success or failure. Taken in its proper context, every act of privatization has the potential for improving economic and social performance; but if recklessly pursued—as is sometimes done—privatization can be a curse more than a blessing. Examples of both scenarios are not hard to find. Our entire discussion is inspired by the need to explore how best to embrace the former, and avoid the latter.

In trying to strike a balance between the public sector and the private sector—to determine the point at which the public sector ends and the private sector begins—a useful point of departure is to understand what lies at the extreme end of each case.

In a free and democratic society, is there a point beyond which government interference in the private lives of its citizens becomes unacceptable? Conversely, is there a point beyond which citizens, whether individually or in groups, must not be allowed to do just as they wish?

These are rhetorical questions. The duly constituted public authority—or government—in every country, has to answer them through laws passed by its own legislature and enforced by its executive and judiciary. Once again, we are in the 'grey area' of society's problems, for which there are no stereotyped solutions. At least in principle, each case has its own unique solution. In the circumstances, the most we can do is to suggest what are the major factors that have to be taken into consideration in reaching an informed decision, and then leave it to those responsible to figure out what weight to attach to each factor to get a realistic answer.

Relevant factors bearing on the situation include (but are not limited to) the following:

- The level of development of a country
- The form of government
- Whether the country has only recently attained independence.

Let us take each in turn.

First, a country's development, both in terms of broad economic prosperity and general enlightenment, is an important, if not a crucial, background factor that determines a meaningful dividing line between the public sector and the private sector. For one thing, the average voter or taxpayer in such a country is unlikely to tolerate excessive interference from the government in his private affairs, just as the government itself, provided its citizens are peaceful and law abiding, would not wish to interfere with the private sector in the first place.

Needless to say, the political environment in such a country is likely to be conducive to the growth of a genuine spirit of democracy, in which the government and the people respect each other's role, and enjoy each other's confidence. In such a situation, whatever responsibilities devolve on the government—in other words, whatever is left to the public sector—is decided by the people themselves, and the same can be said of whatever activities are left in the people's own hands. There is no room for arbitrary action by the public authorities. It is the people themselves who decide what should be the dividing line between the public sector and the private sector.

Few countries in the world quite measure up to this ideal, but the Western democracies of the modern world are probably the nearest approximation to it.

This brings us to the second point, namely, the form of government and its bearing on the privatization debate. I believe it would be fair to say that all non-democratic or authoritarian forms of government—be they monarchies, one-party states, or military dictatorships—are characteristic of regimes that decide, *for* the people, what the limits of their private rights should be. In effect, the private sector of the economy is residually determined, in the sense that its coverage is whatever is left after the state has carved out for itself what it regards as its jurisdictional territory.

The only practical limitation on the government lies, not in its recognition of the legitimate boundaries of its political power—since by definition there is no perception of such boundaries—but only in its human and financial resource capacities. Every dictatorial regime, regardless of its shade or colour, soon discovers that it is 'biting more than it can chew', and decides to offload some of its tasks onto the people.

At the same time, the people themselves, already itching for more political power and the human rights long denied to them, do not hesitate to seize any opportunity that emerges to re-assert themselves, and ask for more. In other words, the scenario we are witnessing is one of an inherent conflict or tug-of-war between the public sector as symbolised by the regime, and the private sector as symbolised by the broad masses of the people.

There is no scientific way to pre-determine the equilibrium point between these two opposed forces, which could enable us to demarcate, as we would wish to do, the proper boundary between the public and the private sectors. All we can say is that, in the end, an equilibrium of sorts will exist, and that will determine for us the dividing line we are looking for.

Unfortunately, before that end is reached, undemocratic societies of this kind could experience any number or manner of political upheavals—from the overthrow of monarchies to repeated military coups and counter-coups. (For proof of this, look no further than the history of African countries a generation after their independence!).

Our third and last point refers to countries that have recently emerged from colonialism. The implication of this is fairly obvious. If experience is any guide, at least a generation or two may pass before newly independent peoples can comfortably shake off their post-colonial 'hang-over'. Memories die hard, and bad memories, harder. Even after years of formal independence, there tends to remain, in most people's minds, a lingering dislike, mistrust, or resentment of the colonialists and what they stood for.

What, you may ask, has privatization got to do with this? At first glace, probably nothing much. But then consider a situation where a government deems it necessary to solicit foreign funds and foreign expertise to manage a privatized project. Its first major task will be to overcome its own people's mental block (beginning with its loyal party followers), to convince them that the return of foreigners to the country is in their own best interests.

Should rumour persist that 'the colonialists are back', then more drastic remedial steps will be necessary to contain it. Basically, this would mean mounting a counter-campaign to cause the people to change their minds—and that is always easier said than done. Before the task is accomplished, considerable expenditure would have to be incurred, to cover such costs as media publicity, mass communications on political platforms, and personal contacts targeted at influential individuals. Regardless of the techniques used, there is no denying the fact that the indirect cost of privatization, however reckoned, will be substantial by the time the post-colonial 'hang-over' has been wiped out.

We may conclude that any privatization which involves the use of foreign resources comes at a price; and the price is higher the greater the post-colonial 'hang-over'. The cost of privatization, in this as in all other cases, has to be weighed against its benefits—bearing in mind that in this particular case political history is a significant factor. This consideration is a pertinent reminder that what is at issue is not simply whether or not to privatize, but at what point in time. It also renders the search for a dividing line between the public sector and the private sector a little more complicated than at first thought, because its determination now acquires a clearly *historical* dimension.

However, it is unlikely that political reorientation alone will be sufficient to produce the desired attitudinal change, and do so quickly enough. For that reason, governments may—and often do—resort to additional measures to cushion any undesirable foreign impact: the aim is to curb the external influence as much as possible, while still attracting foreign skills and capital. As we have indicated elsewhere, one way to do this is by the government retaining a controlling interest in the privatized enterprise, while divesting it to its people at a measured pace. But no matter how you look at it, there is no mistaking the fact that the entire scenario attaches a significant indirect cost element to privatization.

Essay # 6
PRIVATIZATION AND 'FOREIGNIZATION'

The word 'foreignization' is not part of the English vocabulary but, given the subject under discussion, I make no apology for using it, in view of what it has come to connote in most peoples' minds. Language purists may simply substitute the term 'foreign ownership' and read on.

Probably the most cogent argument against privatization, especially in Africa, is that it is tantamount to a change from local ownership to foreign ownership of national resources. Pursue privatization and you usher in foreign ownership or invite neo-colonialism by the back door. While there may be a grain of truth in this argument, it is too often used by unscrupulous politicians to prey on peoples' political sensitivities.

Unfortunately, all too often a government decides that a particular activity should be privatized, but stops short of specifying the exact terms on which privatization should take place. In particular, where the impetus for privatization has a foreign origin, it is important to ensure that it will not take place at the expense of the local population. The most obvious way to do this—although this is an extreme case—is to preclude foreign nationals from the bidding process altogether.

But a more realistic alternative is to invite foreign participation *selectively*, and to limit the quantity of shares they may hold in the privatized company. In the event that the local population is too poor in resources to acquire the required majority of the shares, or lacks the technological know-how and managerial competence needed to run the enterprise, the government may temporarily step in to retain a controlling share in the ownership of the enterprise, until such time as the local citizenry is sufficiently well equipped to take over.

An unwelcome scenario is one in which the enterprise to be privatized is thrown open to foreign bidders, and the successful foreign bidder is promised various concessions, including the repatriation of profits, 'tax holidays,' and other privileges that are denied to local investors. These discriminatory concessions are usually made on the spurious assumption that foreign investment, unless attracted by special inducements, cannot be procured.

Another investment field which has been 'foreignized' to a disturbing degree is the mining sector. Typically, mining enterprises are highly capital intensive. Mineral prospecting alone requires a lot of initial expenditure, and the exploration may take years to bear fruit. Add to this the actual mining operations—the excavation, processing, refining—all of which demand skills as well as capital. The final product then needs to have a profitable market outlet before the initial expenses can be recouped, and surplus profits generated for distribution to shareholders.

Precisely because this big initial investment is not readily available locally, foreign investors can step in virtually on their own terms, listing a long array of risk factors: political uncertainty, large initial capital outlay, possible hostility from the natives in the vicinity of the mines, long gestation period before the investment can be expected to pay off, and so on.

As compensation against these drawbacks, the foreign investor demands—and is often granted—concrete guarantees: a fairly long 'tax holiday', full repatriation of profits, protection against insecurity arising from possible civil strife, a guarantee against take-over or nationalization during the first ten or twenty years of operation. The agreement signed between the government and the foreign investor normally provides for a big and mandatory compensation under international arbitration in the event that it is violated.

It is not surprising that this field is one of the most risky or difficult to privatize, where privatization, in the present context, means the transfer of ownership and management from *foreign* private hands to *national* private hands. This is a case where a workable policy of privatization has to be in two stages: first, the acquisition by the national government of the foreign-owned company; and, second, its acquisition *from* the government by national private entrepreneurs. This two-stage process is necessitated by the fact that the local inhabitants are too poor to buy up the foreign company outright, and must first rely on their own government to do so. The government may rightly be viewed as holding the company in trust for its citizens until such time as the latter are in a position to take it over by themselves.

This defines the path along which orderly privatization should move. The speed and manner of the actual movement is, of course, a separate matter.

Consider the first stage of the process. Foreign-owned or foreign-operated companies, aware of the government's intention to have a controlling interest in the company, as a step towards its early privatization, are careful to ensure that they negotiate the best possible terms they can get—terms which are both secure and lucrative enough for them. The negotiating skills of the foreign entrepreneur have no match on the government's side. Not only are the foreigners better informed about the detailed workings of the company—its strengths and its weaknesses—but their single-minded aim is to maximise profits.

The government side, on the other hand, is no match for them in knowledge, skill, or in motivation. For one thing, their motivation or sense of commitment is much weaker. Just as the welfare of a man and his family is closer to his heart than the welfare of the nation at large, so too does human nature dictate that 'what is good for me' matters more than 'what is good for the country'.

An honest admission of this human frailty—the lack of altruism—would go a long way to explain the incidence of corruption that is so rampant, despite public denials, on the part of government officials who negotiate public contracts with foreign companies! It also goes far to explain the glaring asymmetry that exists between the government side and the company side in the negotiating process.

Essay # 7
PRIVATIZE AT ANY COST?

So far, our discussion points to one inescapable conclusion: privatization is desirable, but only on certain conditions. The reason the subject has remained controversial—and why some people reject privatization outright—is because many of its advocates do not seem to recognize that privatization, to be successful, must meet certain preconditions, failing which the entire exercise may be put in jeopardy.

Some of the desirable preconditions can already be gleaned from the discussion in the preceding essays, and more will emerge when, in a subsequent essay, we review the specific case of privatization in Tanzania. For the moment, let us simply underline a couple of points that are too easily overlooked.

First, let us acknowledge at once that privatization is not an end in itself. Certainly, it is not as if every privatised entity was automatically better than a non-privatized one. There are some private or privatized corporations which, for perfectly understandable reasons, perform worse than they did, or would have done, as public corporations. That is one reason why nationalization (or de-privatization) will always remain a legitimate option on the political agenda.

Second, we must explode the myth that a private enterprise economy (i.e. one in which privatization has been pushed to the extreme) is a manifestation of success in democracy. In fact, enough evidence exists to suggest that the opposite may well be the case. Some private companies, particularly trans-national corporations, have grown so big and so powerful as to undermine both individual freedoms and the sovereignty of democratic governments. Donors who like to equate privatization with democratization, and who insist on progress in privatization in developing countries as a condition for aid, are simply victims of the wrong mindset.

What all this means is that privatization—much like globalization—should not be allowed to proceed unguided. Privatization is not a process from which the public authorities should keep their hands off. On the contrary, it behoves the government of every sovereign state to keep a close watch over the privatization process in much the same way, and for much the same reasons, as it watches over any other national activity—in order to ensure, not only that personal freedoms are not jeopardised, but also that the success of some individuals will not be at the expense of others.

These broad guidelines underscore the need to avoid the blanket application of any single formula—based on the 'one size fit all' mentality—and to zero in on the specifics of each individual act of privatization. They alert us to the fact that the rules that govern privatization in the mineral sector (or a particular mining activity), for instance, need not be the same as those governing privatization in the industrial sector, the agricultural sector, the transport sector, or the tourism sector.

The next thing to bear in mind is that privatization, like any other activity, has a cost—both direct and indirect. A rational decision to privatize is tantamount to an acknowledgement that the expected benefits of the exercise outweigh the expected costs.

But while the benefit side is usually highlighted in the political campaign rhetoric, the cost side is seldom addressed, let alone emphasized. A quick glance at the cost implications is therefore in order.

The *direct* costs of privatization are easy to pinpoint. A private company intending to take over a parastatal corporation must stand ready to incur the expenses necessary for the changeover. These consist of the cost of purchasing the assets and assuming the liabilities of the company, including any outstanding statutory obligations. These costs are incurred directly and paid up front as part of the bidding process.

Other direct costs consist of the necessary expenses that must be incurred to make the business operational as a going concern. The most outstanding among these are the costs of installing a competent management team and a board of directors. Even when it appears desirable to retain some of the existing staff or board members, privatization almost invariably entails big personnel changes, if not a drastic overhaul, in the top managerial echelon; and this has direct cost implications.

To these direct costs may be added the cost of building or hiring office premises, equipment, and securing any necessary supplies, to the extent that they are not part of the pre-existing facilities.

The *indirect* costs of privatization, on the other hand, are often case-specific. They may be high or low, depending on circumstances. In extreme cases, the indirect costs may be prohibitive—enough to rule out privatization altogether as a viable option.

Typically, such costs are hard to quantify and depend largely on the political situation in the country. Is the political atmosphere in general conducive to privatization? Is it friendly or hostile towards the privatization of the activity in question? And, if hostile, what will it take to guarantee security and other protective safeguards, in addition to stimulating productivity?

Among the important indirect costs to be reckoned with are the foreign investment-related costs, already discussed at some length in the preceding essays. In short, whether we are thinking of privatization as a general economic policy, or as an isolated act directed towards a specific enterprise, only a careful analysis of the direct and indirect costs of the exercise will determine whether or not privatization is a paying proposition.

One indirect cost that can have far-reaching economic and social consequences is the effect on employment. Almost invariably, the acquisition of public enterprises by private entrepreneurs leads to significant changes in the size and composition of the labour force. Given the new ownership or body of shareholders, changes in the top managerial echelon are virtually automatic, and a substitution of foreign personnel for local personnel comes as no surprise. Many businesses, once privatized, will replace the entire top and even middle management cadre, and some, unless restrained, may go even further and eliminate the bulk of casual workers and semi-skilled personnel.

Thus privatization tends to create unemployment. The new (especially foreign) owners of a privatized enterprise rationalise their policies in any number of ways: 'downsizing' to reduce overstaffing and cut down on overheads; increasing productivity by hiring a small number of skilled and better-paid workers to replace existing large numbers of poorly trained low-paid casual labourers; utilising modern 'high-tech' equipment which can only be operated by highly trained specialists.

A common tactic used to achieve these aims with minimal disruption is for the new management to initially lay off the whole existing workforce, and require everyone to apply afresh. The intention is to create the impression that everyone is being given a fair chance, though in reality the decision as to who will stay and who will go, together with their pay packages and terminal benefits, may turn out to have long been predetermined.

The final picture (of 'successful' privatization) may look something like this: a preponderance of economic undertakings will be owned and managed by private entrepreneurs; at the top certainly, and lower down probably, the enterprises will be staffed by foreign nationals; and in practically every enterprise, many local workers will have been dismissed.

Taking the private sector as a whole, total employment will have dropped, though average income—judged by income per employed worker—may have risen significantly. Along with a noticeable increase in the foreign presence in the country, which will now be occupying the top echelon of the economy in practically every sector, general unemployment will have risen, and the gap between rich and poor widened. There might be more cars in the streets, more high rises in the city, and more tourist hotels, but also more poverty! All this will have implications for the country's political stability and future economic development—all of which are beyond the scope of our current discussion.

Essay # 8
PRIVATIZATION: OWNERSHIP vs MANAGEMENT

The distinction between the ownership and the management of corporate enterprises is of direct relevance to the subject under discussion. Privatization does not automatically mean the privatization of the ownership as well as the management of an enterprise. It is always possible, and sometimes desirable, to privatize the management of an enterprise while leaving the ownership in public hands (However, the converse is not true: seldom or never will you find a privately-owned enterprise being run by the government!)

It is therefore worth examining briefly the circumstances under which—and the extent to which—it pays to entrust the management of a public corporation to private entrepreneurs.

Actually, this is fairly common practice, and for reasons that are not far to seek. Take the case of public utilities, for example. As one might expect, the ultimate responsibility for ensuring the provision of public utility services—such as water, electricity, transport and telecommunications—rests with the government, not necessarily as the supplier, but certainly as the overseer or guarantor, of such services. The government's role in this respect is more or less similar to its role in setting and guaranteeing standards in commerce and industry.

It is therefore naturally to be expected that for the government to be able to play its role as a supplier or guarantor of public utilities, it must retain legal ownership of the utility industries concerned. This truth is easily overlooked due to the fact that many companies that provide utility services in many countries of the world happen to be private companies. What is not always realized is that the terms of their registration, the regulations that govern the conduct of their activities, and the protection they enjoy, are all a recognition of their unique status. These are private companies *with a difference*: they fulfil a public responsibility.

On closer examination, it can be seen that it is in fact the management—and not the ownership—of these companies that is in private hands. The actual ownership of the utilities remains vested in the government, which is what enables it to enforce the regulations and to intervene effectively in cases of emergency or national disaster—arising from natural causes, war, insurrection or terrorism. In this way, the suppliers of these utilities can neither hold the public at ransom because of their 'importance' as providers of essential services, nor can they themselves be held accountable, in times of emergency, for failure to provide those services since the ultimate responsibility for them rests with the government.

The case of public utilities, therefore, epitomises another special scenario of *privatization with a difference*: not only is management in private hands while ownership is in public hands; but the private management itself enjoys special protection in return for its acceptance of special social responsibilities. This would seem to be a special case of collective responsibility or joint partnership between the public sector and the private sector.

The public utility case may be said to occupy one extreme. There are any number of similar intermediate cases, that shade imperceptibly, like a continuum, into the regular privatization scenario, where both ownership and management are in private hands. As for the intermediate cases, nothing is cast in stone: from country to country, or industry to industry, the rules are flexible, and differ more in degree than in kind.

One or two examples may be quoted: for instance, depending on the country, the transport sector—land, marine, or air—sometimes qualifies for treatment as a public utility, and sometimes not. The same is true of financial services, pharmaceutical services, and the like. In the majority of cases, the principal determinants appear to be the level of development and the degree of democratization that a country has attained.

Taking proper cognizance of the dichotomy between ownership and management is a useful reminder of the fact that there is no simple formula for privatization that is applicable to all cases. Starting with an unmitigated public sector at one extreme, through the admixture of public-cum-private utilities, to the other extreme where an unmitigated private sector reigns supreme—the entire spectrum consists of a continuum of pragmatic real-life cases, each of which deserves to be studied, analysed, and evaluated on its own merits.

In all cases, the private sector (and indeed the privatization process itself) possesses one distinctive merit: it symbolises profit-motivated operational efficiency, as well as the freedom of the individual. The public sector, for its part, in whatever degree it may manifest itself, has one single justification, namely, that it is there to safeguard the public interest. Ideally, what is needed is a meaningful combination of the two.

Essay # 9
PRIVATIZATION IN TANZANIA: A CASE STUDY

Tanzania attained its independence from Britain in 1961. As a typical underdeveloped economy just emerging from colonial rule, the country had relatively few enterprises, public or private. At that time, the public sector consisted of little more than the governmental machinery and infrastructure administered by the various ministries. The bulk of the private sector consisted of subsistence farmers and herdsmen, most of whom grew food crops, and some cash crops (especially cotton and coffee), while a few were petty traders.

Foreign-owned private companies were confined to the petroleum sector, the banking and insurance sector, the mineral sector, and the sisal plantations.

The attainment of independence, and the policy of 'Africanization' that came with it, fuelled the need to be free from foreign economic dependence, and ushered in a wave of sweeping nationalizations in virtually every sector of the economy. "From 3 firms in government hands upon independence in 1961, the numbers rose by a combination of nationalizations and new start-ups to 43 in 1966".

Then came the public declaration of 1967 (popularly known in Tanzania as the Arusha Declaration) when the government publicly committed itself to a policy of 'socialism and self-reliance', and the control of the 'commanding heights of the economy'. These high-sounding clichés were no empty slogans. Overnight, the great bulk of foreign-owned private firms in virtually every economic sector in Tanzania were nationalized. By

1979, the number of public corporations—popularly known as parastatals—had reached 380.

As the number of parastatals went on rising, the burden they were imposing on the government budget, and on the national economy, soon became unbearable. By the end of the 1980s, a change in policy had become imperative.

The case of Tanzania is an object lesson for any interested student. Having started from an extreme anti-privatization posture marked by sweeping nationalizations at independence, the country has made a complete U-turn and has now embraced the opposite extreme. Privatization has become the password—an 'open sesame' for the cure of all the country's economic ills. The experiment is still on-going; its success or failure cannot be pre-judged; full judgement must be left to future historians.

The formal beginning of the privatization process in Tanzania can be traced back to 1991 with the establishment of the Loans and Advances Realisation Trust (LART), intended to boost the implementation of the national economic recovery and reform strategy, which began in the mid 1980s. This was followed by the Public Corporation Act of 1992, and by the establishment of the Presidential Parastatal Sector Reform Commission (PSRC) in 1993, which was charged with the responsibility of overseeing the privatization of specific parastatals.

A careful study of the Tanzanian case reveals all the features—positive and negative—of the privatization process, as well as the various forms that privatization can take.

The first lesson to be learnt is that privatization in Tanzania came a trifle too late. The Arusha Declaration, and the wave of nationalizations to which it gave rise, arrived with a bang! No one gave much thought as to the political and economic consequences of such far-reaching changes. There was blind faith in the leadership of the Party. Any criticism, however well-intentioned, was construed as disloyalty to the Party. Once the President—the Father of the Nation—had spoken, that was it!

By the time that a policy reversal—that is, the need to privatize—became evident, the damage had already been done. Too much had been tolerated in the name of Party loyalty, behind the façade of 'socialism and self-reliance'. It was now time to swallow the (bitter) pill.

To begin with, take a look at the loss-making parastatals. Many of them had long lost any semblance of profitability. For many years, they were being sustained wholly by public subsidies. If they had been in private hands, they would long ago have wound up and been declared bankrupt.

A point had now been reached where such enterprises were no longer wanted in the public sector, because the subsidies necessary to sustain them had become an intolerable burden on the taxpayer. But, by the same token, they were equally unwanted in the private sector, because their profitability was either zero or negative. The divestiture or privatization of such parastatals was therefore out of the question: it was simply not a viable option.

There was only one course of action left—to write them off. This came at a considerable price to the nation, a price which could easily have been avoided had the initial act of their nationalization been objectively analyzed and evaluated.

But the Tanzanian experience is not limited to a demonstration of just a few cases of nationalization which happen to have been undertaken impulsively, without prior preparation. There is more to it than that. Judging by the extremely large number of parastatals which, at the start of the privatization exercise, were deemed to be only good for "liquidation or receivership", it is hard to escape the conclusion that the initial act of nationalizing these enterprises was an error, and the decision to keep them so for an entire generation afterwards was a blunder.

According to a recent study, *PSRC Report on Privatization Impact Study* (Philip and Co., 2005), 92 (or 30%) out of 307 parastatal enterprises came under liquidation or receivership, while the bulk of the remainder were privatized via asset sales (28%), or shares (28%). The rest—a mere 14%—was accounted for under various other forms of privatization, such as leasing and management buyouts. The report states that "such a variety of options are in line with evolving approaches to privatization globally".

Now that privatization is well under way, the experiment seems to be progressing rather well, as a learn-by-doing exercise. The political shift from nationalization to privatization, hesitant at first, is now complete. "Consistent with ongoing reforms, Tanzania has redefined the role of the state to that of policy maker, maintenance of law and order, provider of basic social and economic infrastructure and facilitator of economic growth" (Tanzania National Website).

Reportedly, the country is now regarded as one of the most liberal investment regimes in Africa. It was named Africa's best investment promoter during the African Investment Promotion Agencies 2004 Competition, where the Tanzanian Investment Centre received the first prize among 48 African countries that took part.

Nevertheless, Tanzania still has a long way to go. Far from being complacent, it needs to walk the globalization path carefully, and to steer clear of corruption in particular. A high incidence of corruption is the surest way to hold up progress in human development in this or any other country. There is cause for alarm when a highly respected international watchdog like Transparency International says it has "consistently rated Tanzania as one of the worst countries in the world for corrupt business practices".

We may never know—or accept—the criteria used to draw such a conclusion, but ordinary citizens in Tanzania, to say nothing of the news media, know the truth only too well. Look at the number of times, in the course of a trial, that a defendant's file is lost, found, and lost again! This is a crude but credible measure of the incidence of corruption in the country.

A proper study of the Tanzanian case reveals clearly what has gone right, and what has gone wrong, with privatization.

On the positive side, a good many of the newly privatized companies appear to be doing well enough. They are running efficiently and profitably, expanding their businesses, paying handsome dividends to their shareholders, and, not least, replacing the drain of what were once subsidies, by a growing volume of tax payments to the government. Among the companies that fall into this category are cement companies, breweries companies, and the cigarette company.

On the negative side, several companies in the mining sector, and some in the utilities sector, partly because of their ill-negotiated contracts, have become a public liability. It is almost as if the government bears all the risks, while the private investors take all the profits.

Every time the government has discovered—belatedly—that a particular contract offers it a 'raw deal' and, under public pressure, has tried to revoke or renegotiate it, the end-result has invariably been the imposition of severe penalties on itself by international arbitrators. A glace at newspaper headlines across the country confirms that at present Tanzania is awash with corruption scandals connected with such privatization contracts, the worst of which have to do with gold mining, with electric power supply, and with water utility services.

At this writing, Tanzania is right in the middle of the privatization programme, overseen by the Parastatal Sector Reform Commission (PSRC). Much has been learned since 1993 when PSRC was first created, and when the privatization exercise seriously got under way. Apart from combating corruption—which is always easier said than done—what PSRC now badly needs is to build up legal contract-negotiating capacity that could match the skills of the foreign negotiator, and save the nation from committing the kind of costly and humiliating blunders like those of the past.

This plea is made in all seriousness, seeing that there are many important contracts in the pipeline still to be negotiated and concluded. It may well be that by the time this book goes to print, privatization agreements for the National Microfinance Bank, the National Insurance Corporation, and the Tanzania Railways Corporation, among other high-profile enterprises, will have been sealed. This plea is a call for prompt pre-emptive action!

CONCLUDING REMARKS

These concluding remarks are intended to wind up the discussion by emphasizing the main highlights and the tentative conclusions of the privatization debate.

The first point that emerges is that privatization (like its inverse, nationalization) is a *debatable* issue. There is no single formula, or simple solution, that is applicable to all cases. Each case has to be studied on its own merits. Whether privatization helps or hinders, when to undertake it, and in what form—these are all empirical questions to be answered in an institutional and historical context.

Political and ideological, as well as economic, considerations are central to the debate. Nobody should be misled into thinking that the supposed virtues of a free enterprise economy constitute an adequate case for privatization. Likewise, it is necessary to avoid the tacit assumption that every step towards privatization is a step towards democracy.

The real question to be addressed is where, in a given society, the dividing line between the public sector and the private sector ought to be drawn. The foregoing discussion sheds some light on the issue, even if it provides, not the answer, but only an approach to the answer.

A purely political approach which takes no account of economic factors or of the social consequences of privatization, could easily lead to a swing from one extreme to the other. The Tanzanian experience is a case in point. Soon after independence, the government resorted to wholesale nationalizations—or de-privatizations—across all sectors of the economy. Twenty years on, the government realized its mistake, but swung to the opposite extreme, embracing privatization uncritically across the board. No matter how you look at it, Tanzania is learning its lesson the hard way.

Clearly, privatization is not an all-or-nothing proposition. In Tanzania, within a fairly short period of time, the political pendulum has swung from nationalization at one extreme, to privatization at the other. At either end, privatization—or its absence—proved to be a costly mistake. It is now recognized that the optimum solution, to be determined on the basis of an empirical evaluation which balances the costs and benefits of privatization, lies somewhere between these two extremes.

This book has underscored one important point: what is at issue is not just *whether* to privatize, but *what, how,* and at what point in *historical time*. The need to pay particular attention to case-specific scenarios cannot be overemphasized.

THE END

SUGGESTED READING

1. Privatization: A Global Perspective (Edited by V.V. Rama-nadham; Published by Routledge)

2. Privatization. Toward More Effective Government: Report of the President's Commission on Privatization (White House, Washington DC, March 1988)

3. Economic Management in Tanzania (Dirk Bol, N. Luvanga, and Joseph Shitundu; TEMA Publishers, 1997)

4. Eric J. Boss, "Plans, Promises and Problems with Privatization in Tanzania" (Sokoine University, Tanzania, 2003)

5. Development Challenges and Strategies for Tanzania. An Agenda for the 21st Century (Edited by Lucian A. Msambichaka, Humphrey P.B.Moshi, and Fidelis P. Mtatifikolo; Dar es Salaam University Press, 1994).

ABOUT THE AUTHOR

Peter Eliezer Temu graduated in 1974 from the Food Research Institute of Stanford University, California, with a PhD in the economics of agricultural marketing. A national of Tanzania, Dr. Temu spent his first ten years (1963-1973) in teaching and research: in Kenya, as Economics Tutor at the College of Social Studies, and then as Research Fellow at the Institute of Development Studies, University of Nairobi; and in Tanzania, as Director of the Economic Research Bureau, University of Dar es Salaam.

From 1974 to 1977 he served as National Planning Controller in the Tanzanian Ministry of Finance and Planning, and later as Director of the Institute of Finance Management in Dar es Salaam.

For over 19 years, from 1977 until his retirement in 1996, Dr. Temu worked for the United Nations as a professional economist, at various duty stations; devoting half his time to the United Nations Economic Commission for Africa (in Addis Ababa and Lusaka), and half to the United Nations World Food Council (in Rome and New York).

978-0-595-47753-1
0-595-47753-4

www.ingramcontent.com/pod-product-compliance
Lightning Source LLC
Chambersburg PA
CBHW021043180526
45163CB00005B/2268